HIGH VOICE

12 SACRED VOCAL SOLOS
FOR CLASSICAL SINGERS

ISBN 978-1-4584-1380-2

G. SCHIRMER, *Inc.*

DISTRIBUTED BY

HAL•LEONARD®
CORPORATION

7777 W. BLUEMOUND RD. P.O. BOX 13819 MILWAUKEE, WI 53213

www.schirmer.com
www.halleonard.com

CONTENTS

Pianist on the CD:
Laura Ward

AIN'T GOT TIME TO DIE

Words and Music by
Hall Johnson
piano accompaniment by John Purifoy

Adapted as a solo for this edition.

when I'm heal-in' de sick, _____ when I'm

heal-in' de sick, _ I'm prais - in' my Je - sus, Ain' got time to die. 'Cause _ it takes

all o' ma time _ to praise my Je - sus, all o' ma time to praise my Lord. If

I don' praise _ Him de rocks gon - ter cry out, "Glo - ry an' hon - or,

*Sing: Glorian hon-nuh!

glo - ry an' hon - or!" Ain' got time to die. Lord, ___ I keep so bus - y work -

- in' fer de King - dom, keep so bus - y work - in' fer de King - dom, keep so bus - y work -

- in' fer de King - dom, Ain' got time to die. 'Cause when I'm feed - in' de po', ___

___ when I'm feed - in' de po', ___ when I'm feed - in' de po', __ I'm work-

6

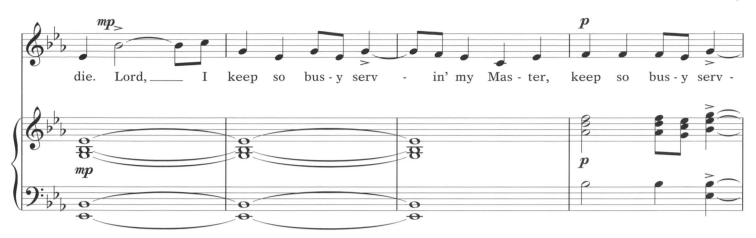

die. Lord, ___ I keep so bus-y serv - in' my Mas-ter, keep so bus-y serv -

- in' my Mas - ter, keep so bus-y serv - in' my Mas - ter,

Ain' got time to die. 'Cause when I'm giv-in' my all, ___

___ when I'm giv-in' my all, ___ when I'm

givin' my all, __ I'm serv - in' my Mas - ter, Ain' got time to

die. 'Cause __ it takes all o' ma time __ to praise my Je - sus,

all o' ma time __ to praise my Lord. If I don' praise __ Him de

rocks gon - ter cry out, "Glo - ry an' hon - or, glo - ry an' hon - or!"

Ain' got time to die. Now, won't you git out o' ma way,— lem- me

praise ma Je - sus? Out o' ma way!— Let - me praise my Lord. If

I don' praise Him de rocks gon-ter cry out, "Glo-ry an' hon - or,

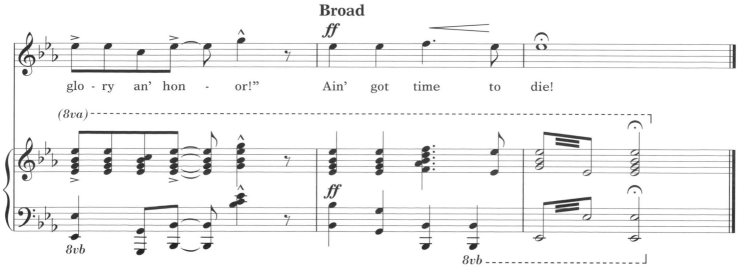

glo-ry an' hon - or!" Ain' got time to die!

AVE MARIA

Franz Schubert

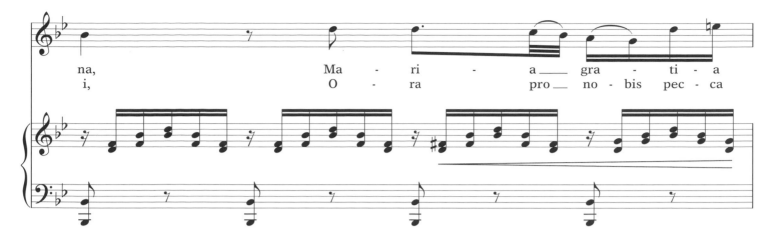

dic - ta tu in mu - li - e - ri - bus, et in
et in ho - ra _____ mor - tis, in

be - ne - dic - tus, et
ho - ra mor - tis no - strae, in

be - ne - dic - tus fruc - tus ven - tris, ven - tris
ho - ra mor - tis, mor - tis no - strae, in

tu - i, Je - sus.
ho - ra mor - tis no - strae.

A - ve Ma - ri - -
A - ve Ma - ri - -

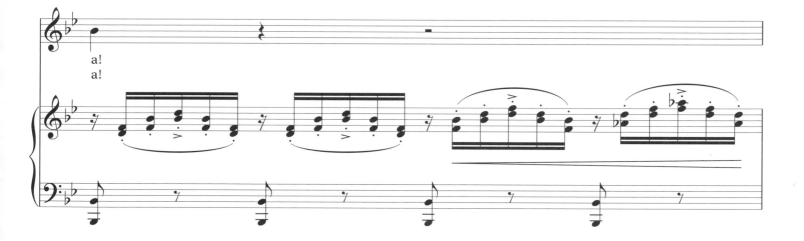

a!
a!

sim.

dim.

BE THOU MY VISION

Ancient Irish
translated by Mary E. Byrne, 1905
versified by Eleanor H. Hull, 1912

Traditional Irish Melody
arranged by Joel K. Boyd

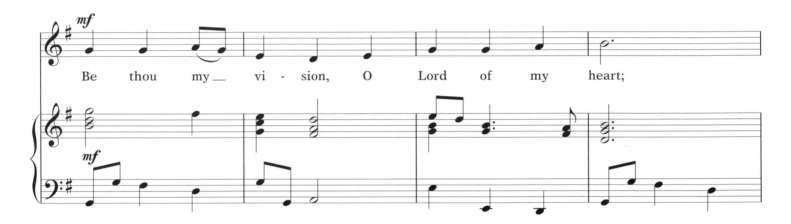

Be thou my vi - sion, O Lord of my heart;

Naught be all else to me, save that thou art:

Thou my best thought, by day or by night,

Wak - ing or sleep - ing, thy _ pres - ence, my light. _____

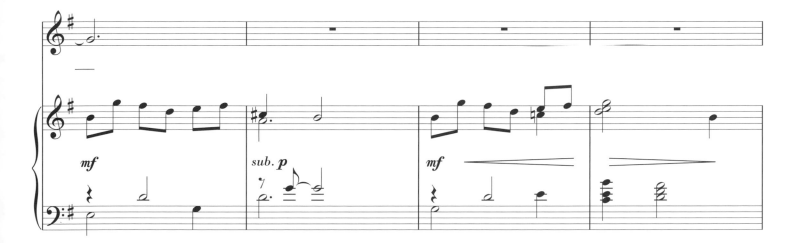

Be thou my _ wis - dom, and thou my true word;

I ev - er with thee and thou with me, Lord:

Thy my_ great Fa - ther, and I thy true son;_____

Thou in me dwell - ing and_ I with thee one._____

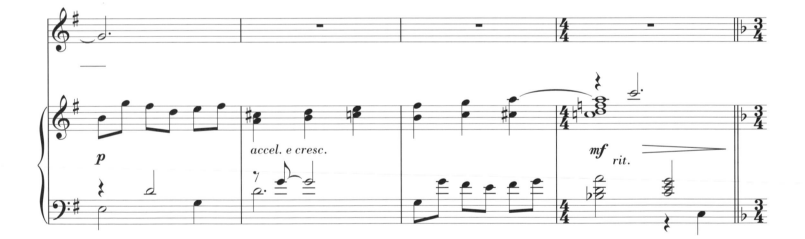

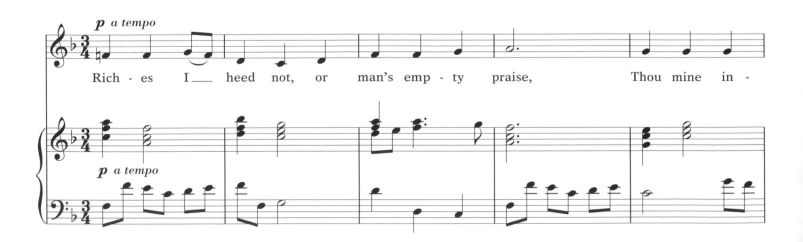

Rich - es I_ heed not, or man's emp - ty praise, Thou mine in -

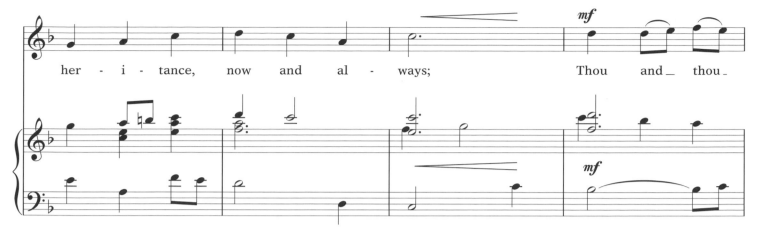

her - i - tance, now and al - ways; Thou and — thou —

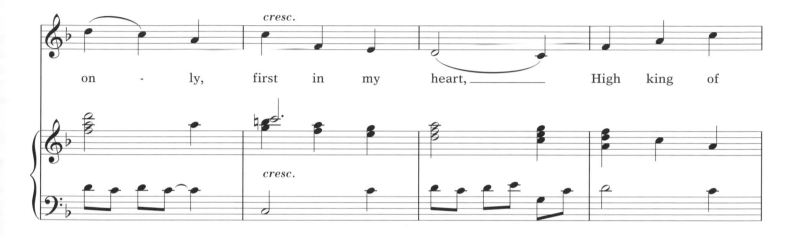

on - ly, first in my heart,_____ High king of

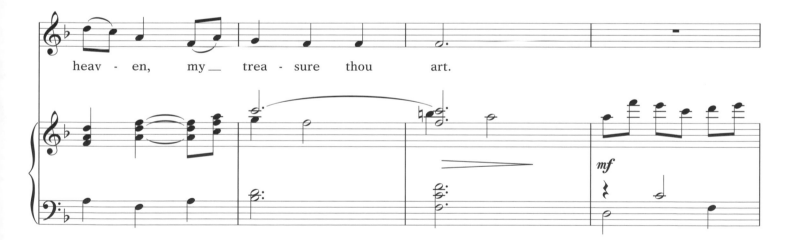

heav - en, my — trea - sure thou art.

Meno mosso

High king of — heav - en, my

victo - ry won, May I reach heav - en's joys, O bright heav'n's sun!

Heart of — my — own heart, what - ev - er be - fall, _____

Still be my vi - sion, O — ru - ler of all. _____

COME SUNDAY

Spiritual from *Black, Brown and Beige*

Duke Ellington
adapted by Lawrence Rosen

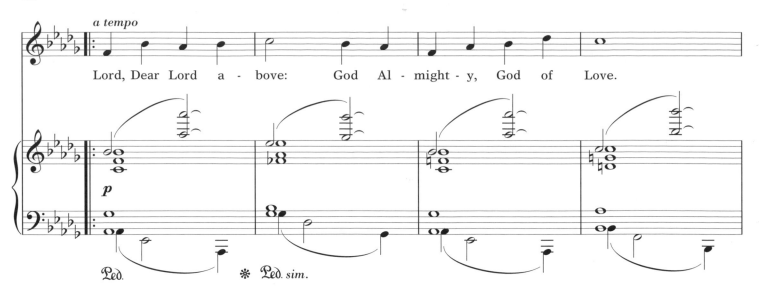

Lord, Dear Lord a - bove: God Al - might - y, God of Love.

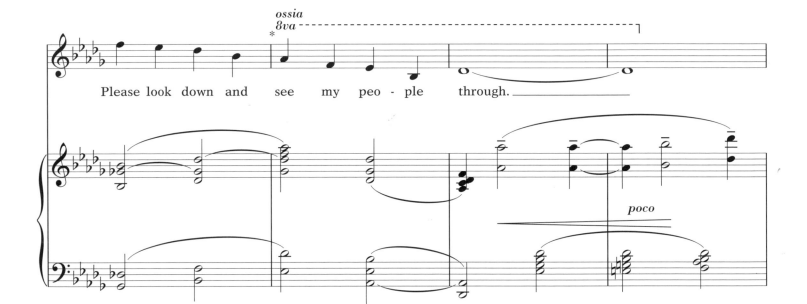

Please look down and see my peo - ple through. _____

1. I be - lieve that God put sun and moon up in the
2. Heav - en is a good - ness time, a bright - er light on

*Alternate rhythm: ♩ ♩ ♩. ♪

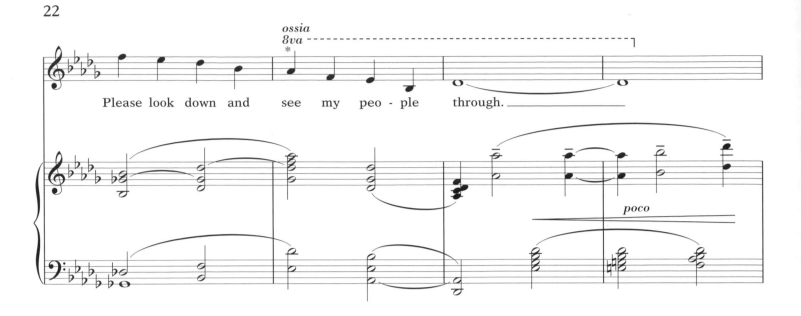

Please look down and see my peo - ple through.

più poco animato

I be - lieve God is now, was then and al - ways will be.

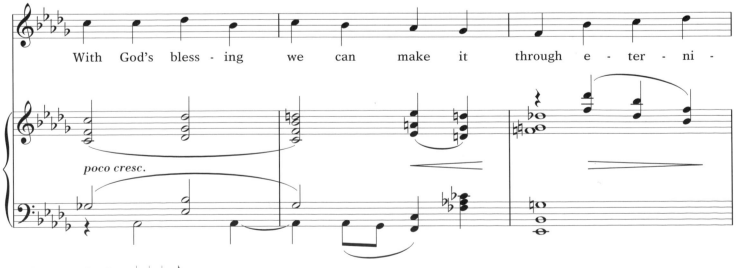

With God's bless - ing we can make it through e - ter - ni -

Alternate rhythm: ♩ ♩ ♩. ♪

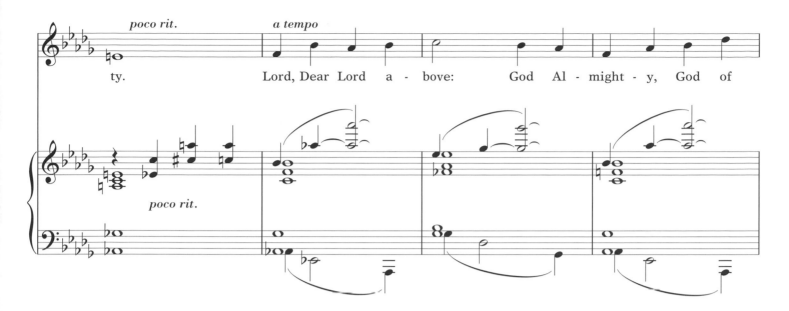

ty. Lord, Dear Lord a - bove: God Al - might - y, God of

Love, Please look down and see my peo - ple through.

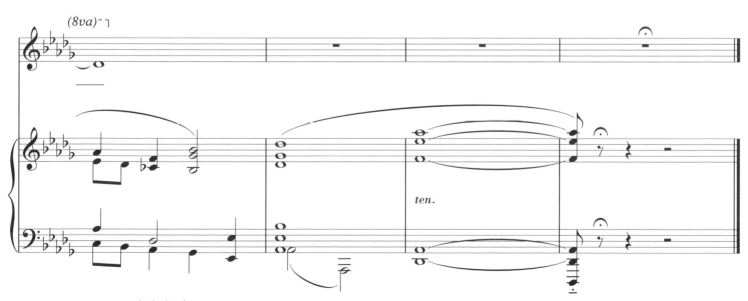

ten.

* *Alternate rhythm:* ♩ ♩ ♩. ♪

CREATE IN ME A CLEAN HEART, O GOD

Psalm 51: 10-13

Carl Mueller

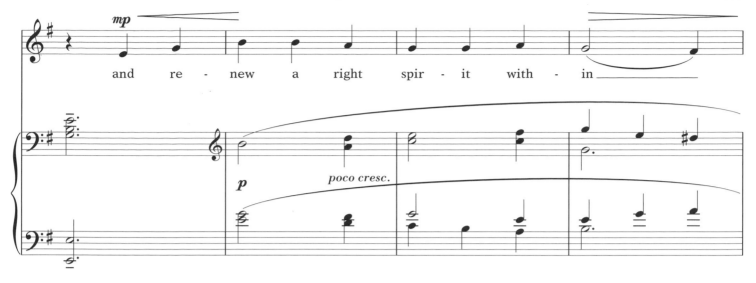

and re - new a right spir - it with - in ____

me.

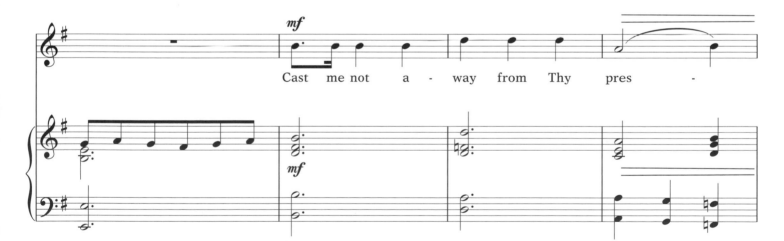

Cast me not a - way from Thy pres -

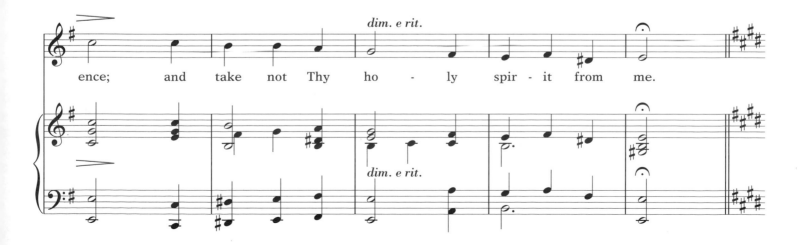

ence; and take not Thy ho - ly spir - it from me.

Poco animato

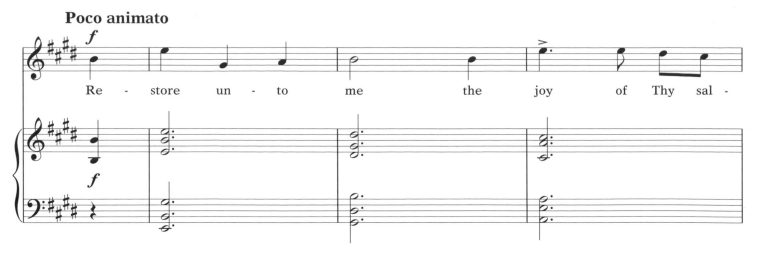

Re - store un - to me the joy of Thy sal -

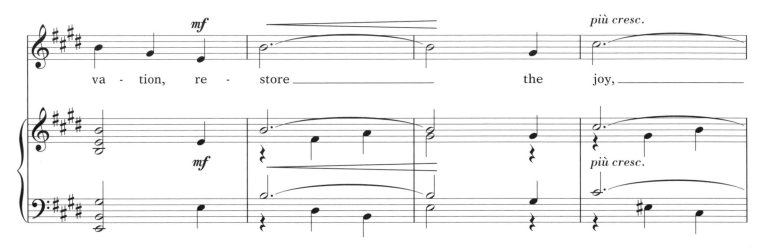

va - tion, re - store _____ the joy, _____

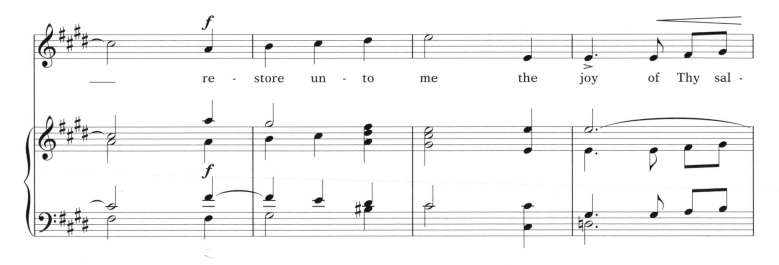

re - store un - to me the joy of Thy sal -

va - tion; and up - hold _____ me, up - hold _____

me with Thy free _____ spir - it, Thy free _____

Moderato

spir - it. Then will I teach trans - gres - sors Thy

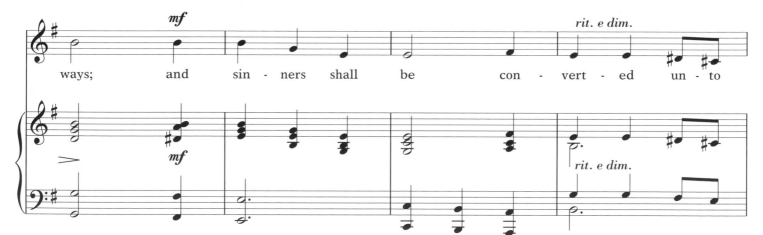

ways; and sin - ners shall be con - vert - ed un - to

Più lento

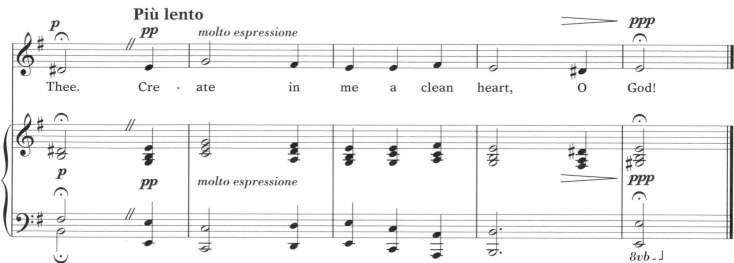

Thee. Cre - ate in me a clean heart, O God!

"Overlook Acre"
Little Silver, N.J.
July, 1956

MY LORD, WHAT A MORNIN'

African-American Spiritual
arranged by Hall Johnson

With mystic expectation

The musical form of this edition has been slightly adapted from Johnson's original.

fall.   *f* 1. You'll hear de trum - pet soun'   To wake de
mf 2. You'll hear de sin - ners moan   To see de

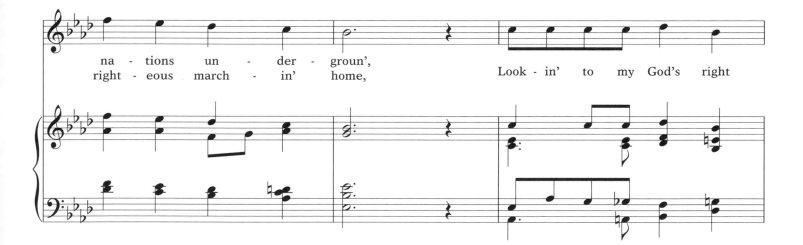

na - tions un - der - groun',   Look - in' to my God's right
right - eous march - in' home,

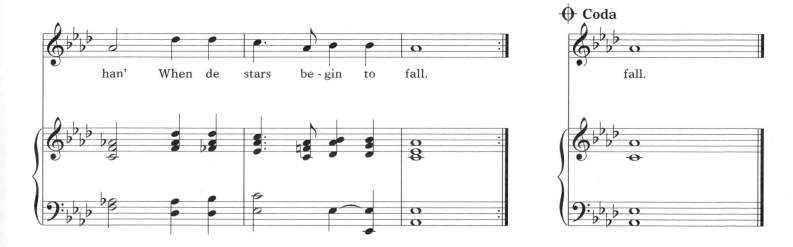

han'   When de stars be - gin to fall.   fall.

Coda

PANIS ANGELICUS

César Frank

ge - li -cus   fit   pa - nis   ho - mi-num,

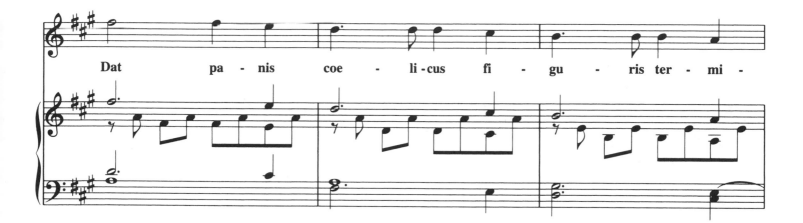

Dat   pa - nis   coe - li -cus fi - gu - ris ter - mi -

num.   O res mi - ra - bi -lis

man - du - cat Do - mi-num,   Pau - per,

pau - per, ser - vus et hu - mi - lis,

Pau - per, pau - per, ser - vus et hu - mi -

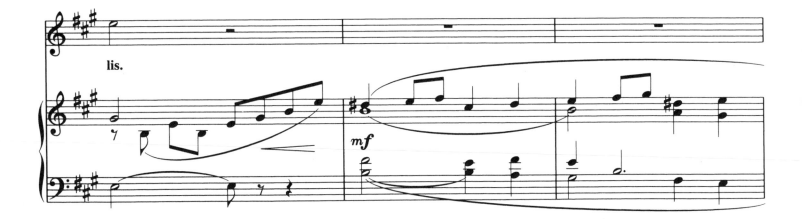

lis.

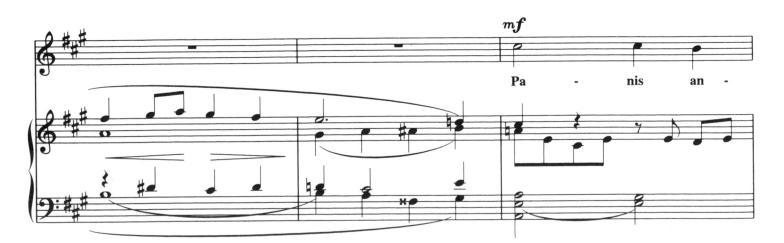

Pa - nis an -

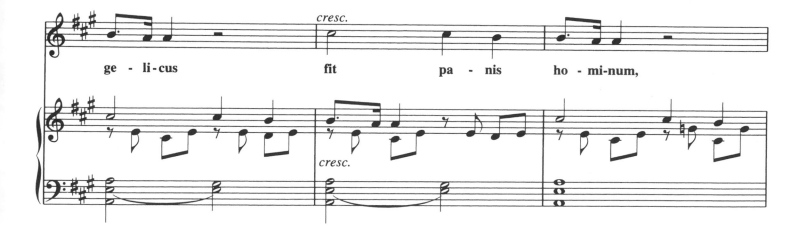

ge - li -cus   fit   pa - nis   ho - mi -num,

Dat   pa - nis   coe - li -cus   fi - gu - ris ter - mi -

num.   O   res   mi - ra bi - lis,

man - du - cat Do - mi-num   Pau - per, __

pau - per, ser - vus et hu - mi - lis,

ff

Pau - per, __ pau - per, ser - vus, __ ser - vus et

hu - mi - lis.

decresc.

p

gratefully dedicated to my friend John Charles Thomas

THE LORD'S PRAYER

Albert Hay Malotte

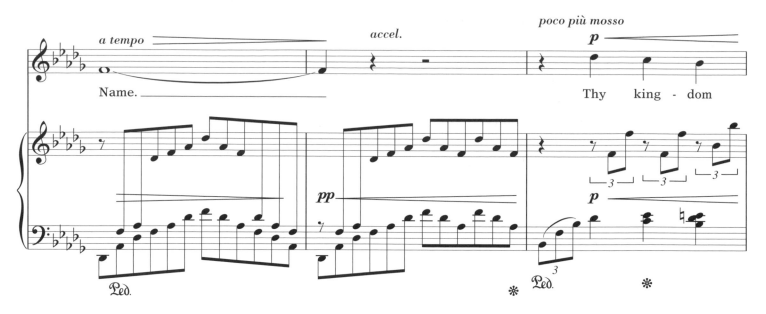

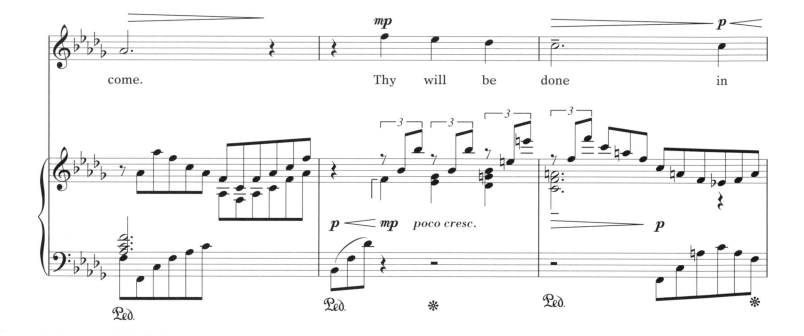

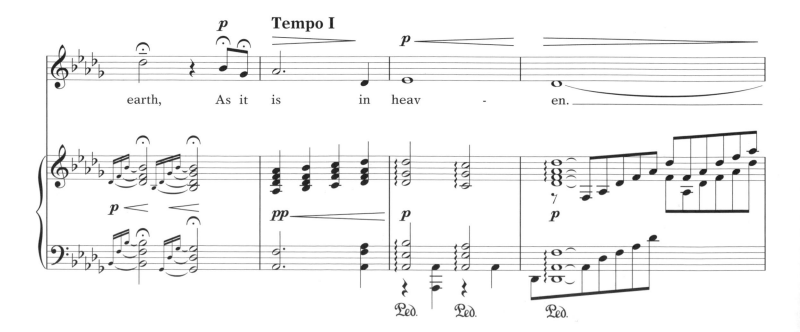

L'istesso tempo

pp molto espressivo e sempre legato

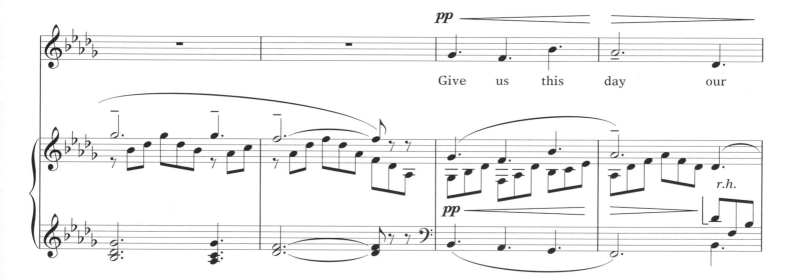

pp

Give us this day our

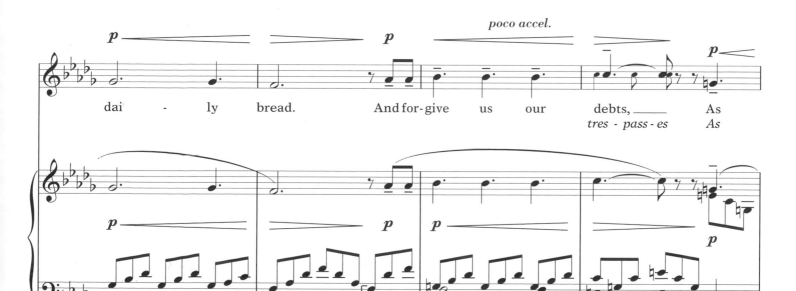

dai - ly bread. And for-give us our debts, ____ As
tres - pass - es As

poco accel.

we _____ for-give our debt - ors.
we for-give those who tres-pass a - gainst us.

And lead us not in - to temp-ta - tion; But de - liv - er us from

Poco meno mosso, e sonoramente

e - vil: For thine is the king - dom, _____ and the

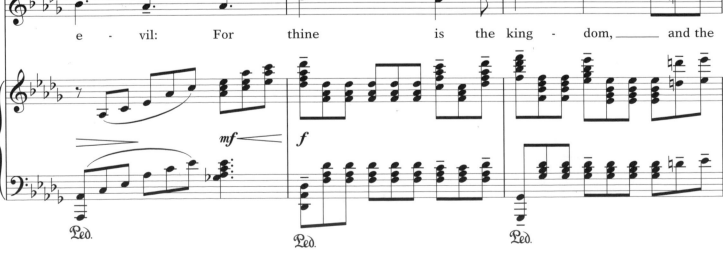

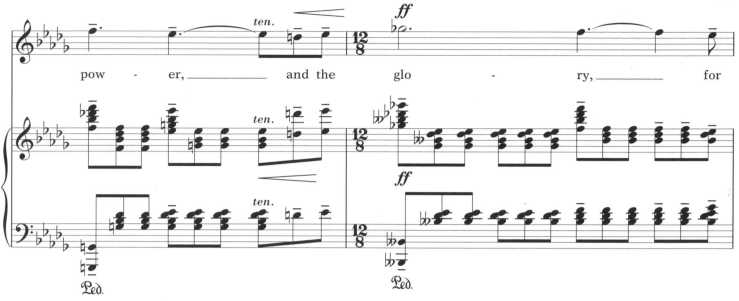

pow - er, _____ and the glo - ry, _____ for

ev - er. _____ A and ev - er. A -

Tempo I

rallentando e morendo

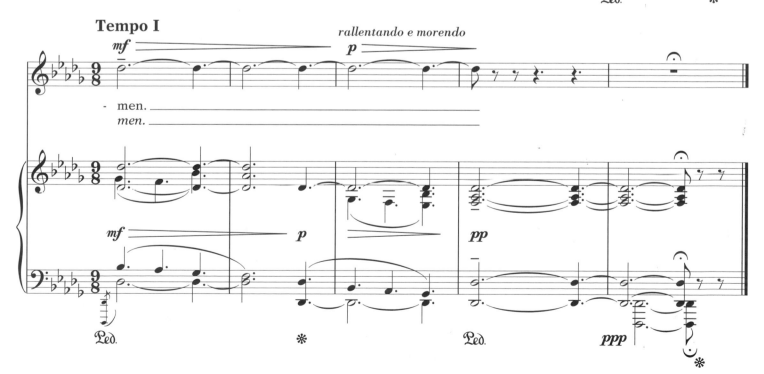

- men. _____
men. _____

PRAISE THE LORD! YE HEAVENS, ADORE HIM

Anonymous

Hyfrydol
Rowland Prichard
arranged by Joshua Parman

stars ___ of light. Praise the Lord! ___ for

He hath spo - ken; Worlds His might - y voice ___ o -

beyed; Law ___ which nev - er shall ___ be bro - ken

For their guid - ance hath He made.

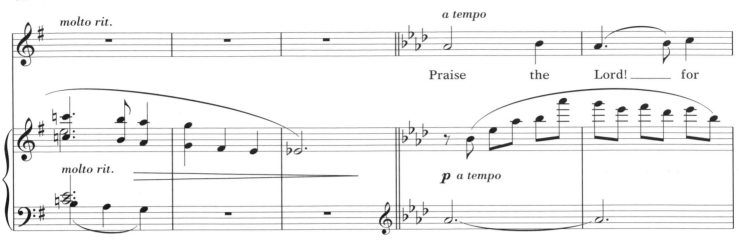

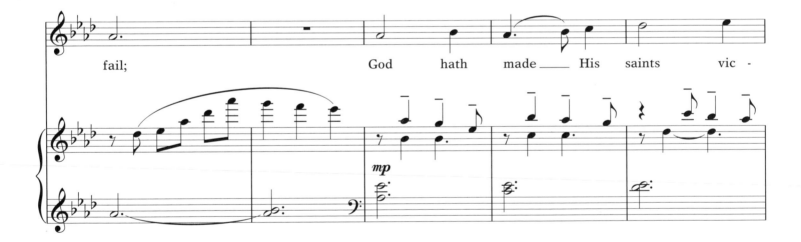

Praise the God of our sal-va-tion! Hosts on high, His pow'r pro-claim; Heav'n and earth and all cre-a-tion Laud and mag-ni-fy His name.

PRAYER OF THE NORWEGIAN CHILD

Olaf Trojörgson

Richard Kountz

Poco più mosso

Je - sus. Lord Je - sus, think on me;
Je - sus.

Make my soul like un - to Thee. Lord Je - sus,

think on me; Make my soul like un - to Thee.

like un - to Thee.

THERE IS A BALM IN GILEAD

African-American Spiritual
arranged by Hall Johnson

The musical form of this edition has been slightly adapted from Johnson's original.

soul. 1. Some - times I feel dis - cour - aged And

think my work's in vain, But then the Ho - ly

Spir - it re - vives my soul a - gain.____ There __ is a

Refrain

balm in Gil - e - ad To make the wound - ed

whole. ___ There _ is a balm in Gil - e - ad To

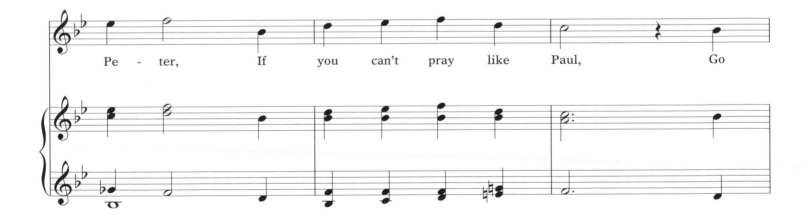

heal the sin - sick soul. 2. If you can't preach like

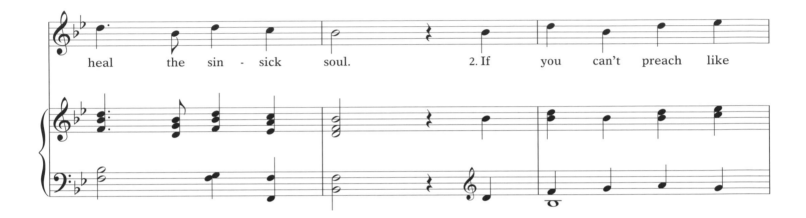

Pe - ter, If you can't pray like Paul, Go

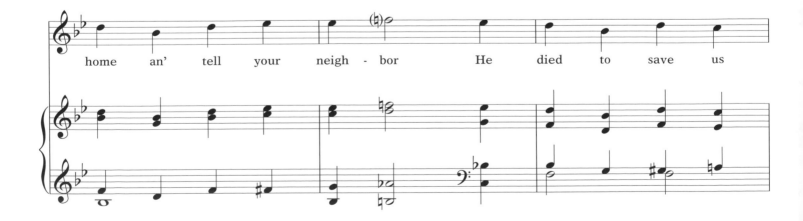

home an' tell your neigh - bor He died to save us

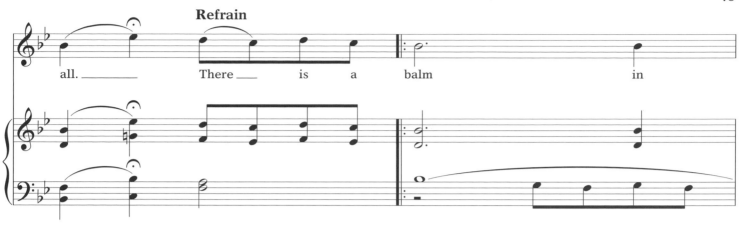

all. ____ There ____ is a balm in

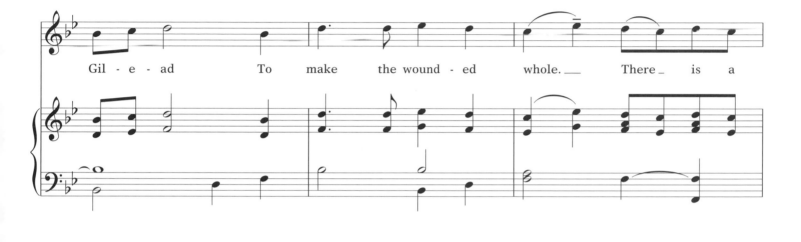

Gil - e - ad To make the wound - ed whole. ____ There ____ is a

balm in Gil - e - ad To heal the sin - sick

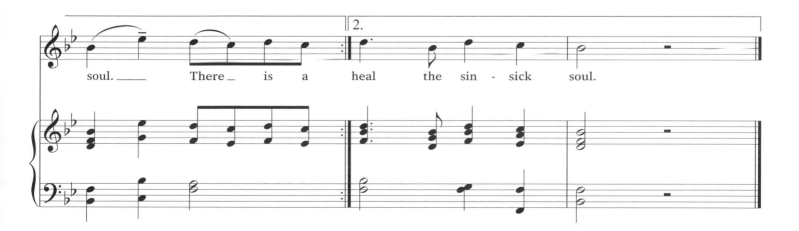

soul. ____ There ____ is a heal the sin - sick soul.

THE 23RD PSALM

Albert Hay Malotte

Quietly and peacefully ($\quarternote$ = 72)

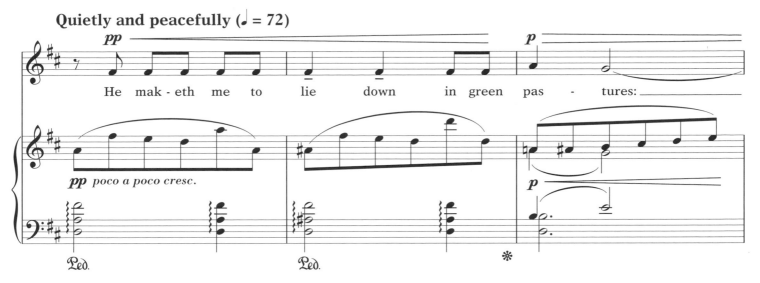

He mak-eth me to lie down in green pas-tures:

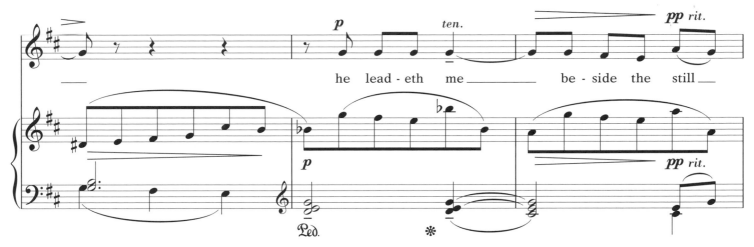

he lead-eth me be-side the still wa-ters. He re-stor-eth my

soul: He lead-eth me in the paths of right-eous-ness for

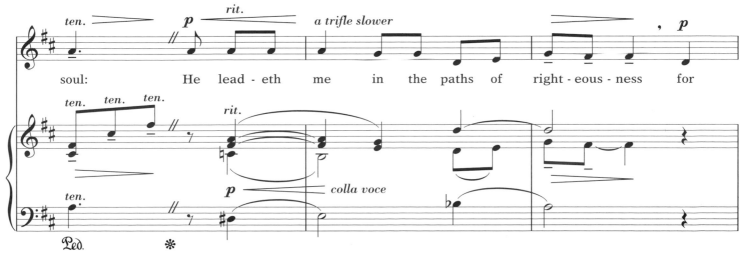

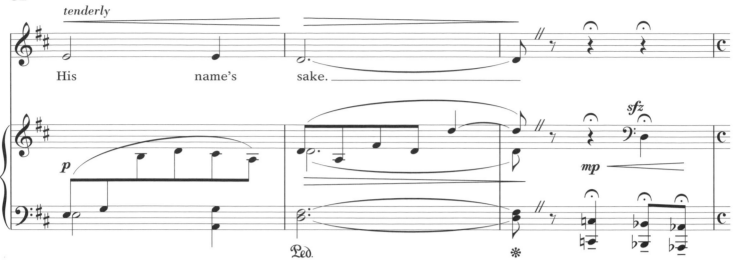

tenderly

His name's sake.

Adagio (mournfully)

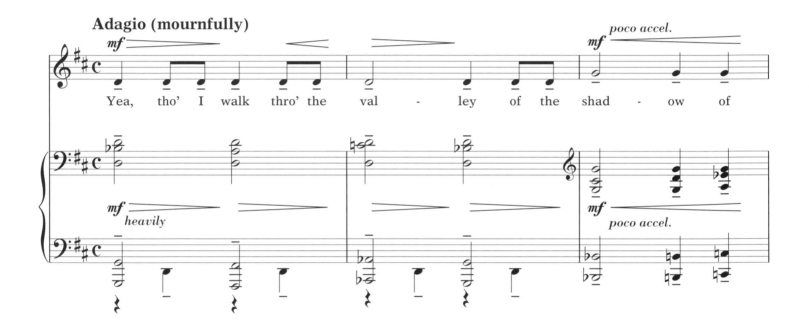

Yea, tho' I walk thro' the val - ley of the shad - ow of

heavily

poco accel.

Suddenly much faster (with conviction)

death, I will fear no e - vil: for

sostenuto

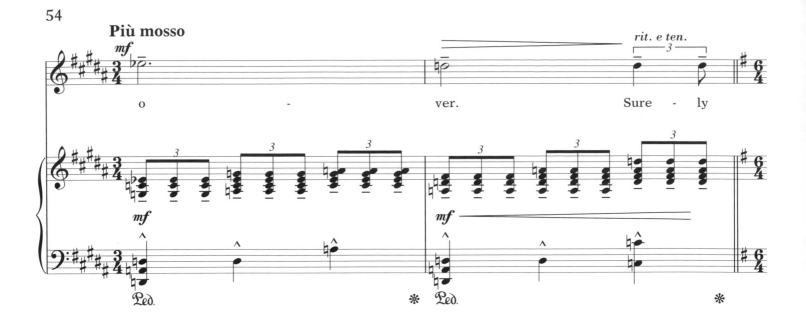

Più mosso

o - ver. Sure - ly

Allegro moderato (joyously)

good - ness and mer - cy shall fol - low me

all ___ the days of my life: ___ and I will

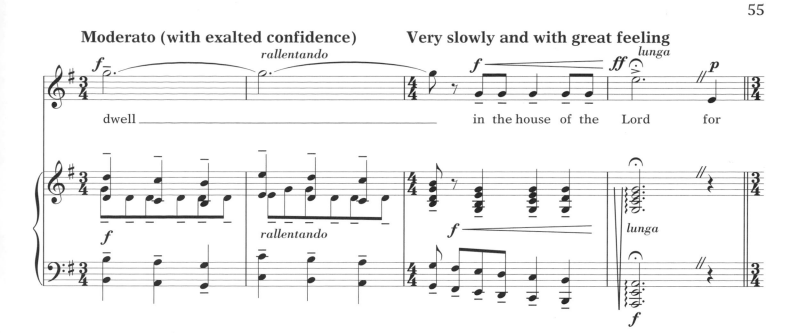

Moderato (with exalted confidence)   **Very slowly and with great feeling**

dwell _____ in the house of the Lord for

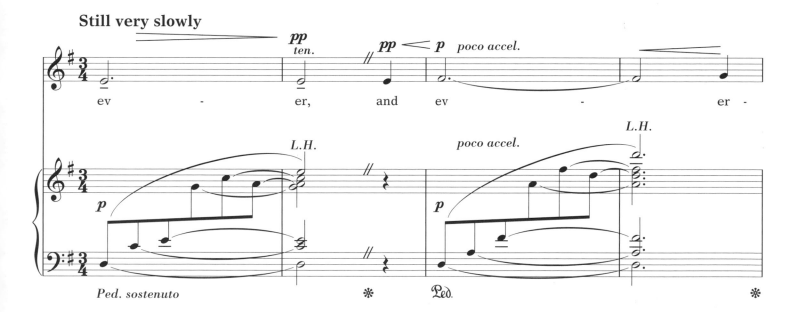

Still very slowly

ev - er, and ev - er -

Ped. sostenuto

Tempo Iº (♩ = 72)

more. _____

About the Enhanced CD

In addition to piano accompaniments playable on both your CD player and computer, this enhanced CD also includes tempo and pitch adjustment software for computer use only. This software, known as the Amazing Slow Downer, was originally created for use in pop music to allow singers and players the freedom to independently adjust both tempo and pitch elements. Because we believe there may be valuable educational use for these features in classical and theatre music, we have included this software as a tool for both the teacher and student. For quick and easy installation instructions of this software please see below.

In recording a piano accompaniment we necessarily must choose one tempo. Our choice of tempo, phrasing, ritardandos, and dynamics is carefully considered. But by the nature of recording, it is only one choice. Similar to our choice of tempo, much thought and research has gone into our choice of key for each song.

However, we encourage you to explore your own interpretive ideas, which may differ from our recordings. This new software feature allows you to adjust the tempo up and down without affecting the pitch. Likewise, the Amazing Slow Downer allows you to shift pitch up and down without affecting the tempo. We recommend that these new tempo and pitch adjustment features be used with care and insight. Ideally, you will be using these recorded accompaniments and the Amazing Slow Downer for practice only.

The audio quality may be somewhat compromised when played through the Amazing Slow Downer. This compromise in quality will not be a factor in playing the CD audio track on a normal CD player or through another audio computer program.

INSTALLATION FROM DOWNLOAD:

For Windows (XP, Vista or 7):
1. Download and save the .zip file to your hard drive.
2. Extract the .zip file.
3. Open the "ASD Lite" folder.
4. Double-click "setup.exe" to run the installer and follow the on-screen instructions.

For Macintosh (OSX 10.4 and up):
1. Download and save the .dmg file to your hard drive.
2. Double-click the .dmg file to mount the "ASD Lite" volume.
3. Double-click the "ASD Lite" volume to see its contents.
4. Drag the "ASD Lite" application into the Application folder.

INSTALLATION FROM CD:

For Windows (XP, Vista or 7):
1. Load the CD-ROM into your CD-ROM drive.
2. Open your CD-ROM drive. You should see a folder named "Amazing Slow Downer." If you only see a list of tracks, you are looking at the audio portion of the disk and most likely do not have a multi-session capable CD-ROM.
3. Open the "Amazing Slow Downer" folder.
4. Double-click "setup.exe" to install the software from the CD-ROM to your hard disk. Follow the on-screen instructions to complete installation.
5. Go to "Start," "Programs" and find the "Amazing Slow Downer Lite" application. Note: To guarantee access to the CD-ROM drive, the user should be logged in as the "Administrator."

For Macintosh (OSX 10.4 or higher):
1. Load the CD-ROM into your CD-ROM drive.
2. Double-click on the data portion of the CD-ROM (which will have the Hal Leonard icon in red and be named as the book).
3. Open the "Amazing OS X" folder.
4. Double-click the "ASD Lite" application icon to run the software from the CD-ROM, or copy this file to your hard drive and run it from there.

MINIMUM SOFTWARE REQUIREMENTS:

For Windows (XP, Vista or 7):
Pentium Processor: Windows XP, Vista, or 7; 8 MB Application RAM; 8x Multi-Session CD-ROM drive

For Macintosh (OS X 10.4 or higher):
Power Macintosh or Intel Processor; Mac OS X 10.4 or higher; MB Application RAM; 8x Multi-Session CD-ROM drive